Five
Little
Christmas
Dramas
for Today's Kids

Timothy W. Ayers

CSS Publishing Company, Inc.
Lima, Ohio

FIVE LITTLE CHRISTMAS DRAMAS FOR TODAY'S KIDS

FIRST EDITION
Copyright © 2014
by CSS Publishing Co., Inc.

For more information about CSS Publishing Company resources, visit our website at www. csspub.com, email us at csr@csspub.com, or call (800) 241-4056.

e-book:
ISBN-13: 978-0-7880-2796-3
ISBN-10: 0-7880-2796-4

ISBN-13: 978-0-7880-2795-6
ISBN-10: 0-7880-2795-6

PRINTED IN USA

This book is dedicated to my wife, Marylee, who has to read and edit everything. My grandsons, Jude, Cameron, and Zachary because they drive my mind to stay current and to make sure that I can talk "kid." Scott and Joni McCagg, who had to put on these plays and help me refine the production quality. The Hill family, who got roped into every production. The Hausauers, from Gramma and Grampa down to the smallest one who threw their whole hearts and talents into each play. All the children of my small western New York church, who made me proud and allowed me to see my words come to life.

Foreword

It comes every year to small churches all across the world. As much as the congregation loves to see those sweet, little children of the Sunday school in a church play, they have no idea what a grueling job it is to produce. The toughest part is selecting a play that the kids will like and want to perform. My first two years at my small church, I watched plays completely devoid of any connection to things kids like or would watch. I got frustrated and decided to write our own plays. We were a small church with about a dozen kids with an age spread from kindergarten to junior high. The first play was about a Christmas play rehearsal. Honestly, I just took the mayhem I saw the year before and wrote it into a script. Everyone loved it because it was what we all knew Sunday school Christmas plays were really like behind the scenes. The children loved it because they were playing themselves. That is the secret to good acting.

The second one was the toughest. I needed a new idea so I did some research: I went to toy stores. Voila! There it was in front of me — toys. Imagine that! I saw toys at a toy store. *Joy Story* was born. The kids had a blast. Characters changed as we found readily available costumes. The children had their own ideas of what character they wanted to be. The kids took ownership and even developed their own characters. Mothers came with old Halloween and school costumes. My favorite was a dinosaur. We put our youngest, very active child in it and let him run around until his "batteries" waned. It was a fluid process. We allowed the kids to have an active part in making the Christmas play their own.

The third play came from a long-held desire of mine to do a take-off of the *Christmas Carol* by Charles Dickens. *Almost, Just Like Dickens' Christmas Carol* is a kid's version of the book. The characters are a little more restricted but the dialogue has lots of room for your own funny lines to be added. I also wrote this one because most small churches have that one child, either boy or girl, that is destined for the stage or big screen. Abby (or Andy) is written just for them.

Don't be afraid to add your own humor and your own church's "inside jokes." Those jokes make the play your own. Don't worry about retelling the story in a perfect way. Everyone knows the *Christmas Carol* story but not everyone gets a chance to hear it in a fresh, new way.

The fourth play in this collection is called *The "I Hate Christmas" Club*. Sometimes, even we adults get the meaning and purpose of Christmas confused. As the lead character expounds on his or her reasons for thinking Christmas is "stupid" (because everything is stupid when you reach a certain age), their counterpart is able to answer with both truth and lessons from the Christmas carols they sing. Although you can add any song that fits to the song choices, I have kept with Christmas carols that are in the public domain. This keeps your cost down and your familiarity quotient high. It has a touching ending and several key insights in to what Christmas is all about.

The last play is titled *Elf Elementary*. Yep, it is just like it says, the kids are playing Santa's elves during an elementary class. Mrs. Claus has come to speak with the children about the truth of Christmas. This one is filled with funny lines and the real story of Christmas.

Now go out and celebrate Christmas in your small church!

(Note from author to the director)

Christmas plays for small churches are sometimes difficult. We are limited by how many children we have and by the usually wide-spread age groupings. I have attempted to write lines that are age appropriate. Feel free to change boys to girls and vice versa. I tried my best to keep gender-specific roles to a minimum. I have added roles that are ideal for the youngest members of the Sunday school. Their lines are simpler and the roles usually have more activity than lines. Lastly, I talked to kids before writing the plays. I wanted to know what they thought was "lame." I usually agreed with them (as long as I wasn't the one who they thought was lame) and that is why my characters are written for today's students.

The set designs are fairly easy. *Joy Story* is most likely the toughest set to produce but a handy parent or grandparent can make the toy box with limited supplies. In a couple of the plays, the set is actually your pulpit platform. I like it simple.

Lastly, try to use as many microphones as possible. Children are loud and noisy when playing but soft and shy when acting (there are a few who are exceptions to this rule). Remind them to use their "outside voices" when delivering a line. Also, have the characters move toward a microphone when they say their lines or place the microphones in key places. Your resident church techie will know what to do.

Table of Contents

Dress Rehearsal for Christmas

Approximate length: 35 minutes

Cast:
Miss Johnson — director
Ms. Emelia VanDerSmooten — pianist (usually played by
the pianist that plays for Sunday school or church)
Pastor
Mr. Johnny — church custodian
Sunday school kids
Suggested ages have been used for different characters but
each part should fit each student.
Teacher
Lora Desmond — a take-off on the Carol Burnett character
of Scarlett O'Hara

Props:
Wrapped boxes for the ending procession
Star costume for a young girl
Donkey costume (costumes can be as simple as a hat with
long donkey ears to a full costume)
Star costume for Mr. Johnny
Elvis costume for Mr. Johnny
Microphone
Camel costume for young boy
Curtain on a rod used as a dress for Lora Desmond — as in
the well-known Carol Burnett skit

(Two boys race out the side door, up the steps, across the platform, through the back side door, and around once more with another boy dressed in a camel suit chasing them.)

Miss Johnson: Boys, stop it. What is going on? We need to rehearse.

Older Boy 1: He says he is a camel and that camels spit. We're running from him.

Older Boy 2: Yeah, camels spit, you know that, Miss Johnson?

Miss Johnson: *(grabs preschool age boy dressed as a camel and stops him)* All right, that is enough of the camel thing. Children, hurry now. We are running out of time and this is our last rehearsal before the big Christmas play. Quickly now. Take your places. We are wasting good practice time.

(The rest of the children race in from all directions and take their places.)

Miss Johnson: Quiet now. *(exasperated, she yells)* Quiet! Remember we are trying to put on a play that reflects the solemn event of the birth of the Christ Child. I need you to put on your serious faces. Let's go.

Older Boy 1: Miss Johnson, I forgot my script.

Older Girl 1: I did too. I forgot my costume as well, and I forgot to do my homework and I didn't eat any supper.

Miss Johnson: Oh please kids, we have to start practice right away. We haven't a moment to delay. Where is Ms. VanDerSmooten, our pianist?

Ms. VanDerSmooten: *(snoring)*

Miss Johnson: *(loudly)* Ms. VanDerSmooten!

Ms. VanDerSmooten: *(begins to play loudly)*

Miss Johnson: *(exasperated)* Not now, Emelia.

Ms. VanDerSmooten: Oh, yes, yes. I was just resting my poor old eyes. We all need our beauty sleep, you know. Where are we, Miss Johnson?

Miss Johnson: We are going to start at the very beginning. I need my narrator. Where is he?

Narrator: *(sheepishly raises hand and whispers)* Here.

Elementary Age Girl 1: You have to be louder than that!

Older Boy 2: Yes! Really loud like this: *(yells)* "About that time Caesar Augustus ordered a census!"

Ms. VanDerSmooten: Which song was that?

Miss Johnson: We didn't ask for a song, Ms. VanDerSmooten. But we will be singing our opening song in a few seconds. Okay, kids, into your places for the opening song. *(surveys the group)* We are missing someone. Where is (Middle School Age Boy)?

Donkey: *(from offstage)* I'm not coming out wearing this.

Miss Johnson: No one has seen it yet. You are one of the most important parts of the play. Come out. The play rides on you.

Mary: Actually, I ride on him into Bethlehem.

Donkey: *(enters wearing the donkey costume)* Do I have to wear this?

Older Girl 1: I think you look nice. It takes a real man to play that part.

Elementary Age Boy: Ee-ahh, Ee-ahh, Ee-ahh

(Donkey shakes a fist at Elementary Age Boy but is laughing at the joke at the same time)

Donkey: I guess you're right. I do look kinda handsome, don't I?

Miss Johnson: First song now. Ms. VanDerSmooten, we are ready for you.

SONG 1 *(Choose a traditional Christmas carol. Most carols are in the public domain, known by everyone, and easy to sing for a small group.)*

When song ends: Enter Mr. Johnny wearing an Elvis costume. He skids to a stop making a big entrance. A male Sunday school teacher works best for this role and brings the entire Sunday school into the production.

Mr. Johnny: Am I on time?

Kids: *(in unison)* Hey, Mr. Johnny. We love the suit.

Mr. Johnny: Thank ya, thank ya very much kids *(in Elvis voice)*. I read in the bulletin that there were try-outs for the part of the king in the play. Well, here I am.

Miss Johnson: *(frustrated and rolls her eyes)* It's the wrong king.

Mr. Johnny: You mean there's another king of rock'n'roll?

Older Boy 2: Elvis was the king of rock'n'roll but this play is about the King of the Jews.

(Mr. Johnny hangs his head in disappointment and kicks at the ground in an "Aw shucks" sort of way.)

Older Boy 1: The king can't leave without singing a song.

Older Girl 2: Yeah, how about "Blue Christmas." That fits this rehearsal fairly well.

Mr. Johnny: Well, since there is such a demand *(turns around with his back to the congregation and strikes an Elvis pose)*.

SONG 2: "Blue Christmas" *(campy version of the song)*

(Older kids decide to be his back-up singers on the woo-ha-woos. If you add some group unison movement this will become a great sight gag.)

Mr. Johnny: Thank ya, thank ya very much. *(exits)*

Middle School Age Boy 1: Ladies and Gentlemen, Elvis has left the building.

(in walks the pastor)

Pastor: How is practice going, kids?

Kids: *(in unison)* Great, pastor.

Donkey: The play is really good, pastor. Wait until you see it.

Pastor: Can't wait. By the way, that is a nice costume. You look quite handsome.

(Donkey smiles and looks proud)

Miss Johnson: We were just going to start. Would you like to stay and watch?

Pastor: I have lots to do for my Christmas message so I will pass and stay out of your way.

Miss Johnson: Thank you, pastor, for stopping by. Now, children, in order to make sure we are doing our dramatic parts correctly I have invited a very famous movie-star from the silent movie era, Miss Lora Desmond.

(all applaud)

Middle School Age Girl: Why were they silent? Couldn't they turn up the sound?

Older Boy 1: I wish this were a silent Christmas play then I wouldn't have to learn all these lines.

Older Girl 1: I wish you were silent.

Older Girl 2: Ditto on that.

Miss Johnson: Please, please, now let's have a round of applause for the star of stage and screen, Miss Lora Desmond.

Lora: Thank you, thank you, my adoring public. I would like to thank everyone in the academy for this award. First of all: my director, then the little people who I have always respected along the way....

Older Girl 1: *(scurries around the platform, finds a microphone, and runs to Lora to do an interview)* Miss Desmond, hi, this is (girl's name) from WCSS (initials of church work great here). I am so excited to be interviewing you for the show.

Lora: Yes, my "After the Oscars" interview. Where is the camera?

Older Girl 1: This way, Miss Desmond *(points to the congregation)*. The biggest question we have as actors is, "What does Christmas mean to you?"

Lora: At one time, in my big, big Hollywood mansion it meant parties, lots of decorated trees, and tons of gifts for me from my adoring public neatly placed under the tree.

Older Girl 1: Has that changed?

Lora: Oh my, yes. So many of the great actors and actresses have gone on to do the big Christmas play in the sky. Today my life is simpler. I decorate one tree and I have the neighborhood kids come over and put presents for the poorer children under the tree.

Older Girl 1: That is a beautiful thought.

Lora: I am beautiful. You are right.

Older Girl 1: Uh, yeah, I guess so. By the way, I love your dress.

Lora: It was just something I had hanging around the house.

Older Boy 1: Ms. Desmond, since you are a famous actress, can you give us kids a few tips?

Lora: *(turns to kids)* Yes, stay out of the stock market and never play in traffic.

Older Boy 2: I think he meant acting tips.

Elementary Age Girl 1: I want to be a great actress like you. *(hugs Lora)*

Elementary Age Girl 2: Me too. *(hugs Lora)*

Preschool Age Girl 3: Me too. *(hugs Lora)*

Lora: Well, kids, it is all in the eyes.

Ms. VanDerSmooten: Ready as can be. *(everyone is startled that she is awake)*

Miss Johnson: You're awake?

Ms. VanDerSmooten: I never sleep when it is show time, Miss Johnson. Especially when Mr. Johnny is on the stage. *(swoons a little)* That guy is real eye candy.

Miss Johnson: Too much information, Ms. VanDerSmooten. Let's get started kids.

SONG 4

(Sunday school teacher enters with Santa Claus — they are carrying stacks of gifts)

Preschool Girl 1: It's Santa!

Preschool Boy 1: Santa!

Preschool Girl 2: I love gifts. Santa is bringing gifts.

Preschool Boy 2: We love Santa, we love Santa… *(all join in with this chant)*

(Miss Johnson raises her hands to stop the chanting)

Sunday School Teacher: Sorry to interrupt you, Miss Johnson, but I got a gift for each kid in the Sunday school. I thought they could open them after the play tomorrow. We were going to set them down under the tree.

Miss Johnson: What else could happen? *(looks at the congregation then lifts eyes toward heaven)*

Older Girl 2: Miss Johnson, some of us kids have been talking and we would like to make a suggestion.

Miss Johnson: Please do.

Older Girl 1: I had a great idea and I think it keeps with the simplicity of the holy event while still showing the excitement and joy people felt at the birth of Christ.

Older Boy 3: Yeah, we need to show more joy and right now none of us are feeling much joy over this play.

Older Boy 2: Christmas needs to be more about giving because Jesus was the gift that God gave us.

Donkey: We need to show people that God is here in our hearts.

Older Girl 1: I guess what we are trying to say is that we can make this play a lot better by making it simpler.

Miss Johnson: What's your idea?

Older Girl 1: Couldn't we just enter from the back of the church and do a simple procession? We can carry the gifts that our Sunday school teacher brought to the front and present them to the Lord.

Older Girl 2: And then later we can take them to poor children who won't be getting anything this Christmas. It would

(Lights up on Eddy and Maggie standing in front of the toy box.)

Mom: *(voice from offstage)* Eddy, Maggie, it is time for bed. Remember tomorrow is Christmas and tonight Santa comes. So you want to get into bed early because you will be up early tomorrow morning.

Maggie: I don't want to go to bed yet, Eddie.

Eddie: Mag we have to. The old toys have been put away and tomorrow we are going to get a whole bunch of new ones. The list I gave Mom and Dad had to be as long as my arm. I'll be opening toys right up until the time we have to go to church.

Maggie: Me too. I hope I get a new dolly. Mine is missing an arm and her dress fits funny now.

Eddie: Where did the arm go?

Maggie: I don't know. It might still be back in the apple grove behind the house. Barbie and I played out there a lot last summer.

Eddie: Barbie?

Maggie: My dolly. Her name is Barbie. Don't boys know anything about toys?

Mom: *(voice from offstage)* Kids! Do I have to count to three? One... two...

Eddie: Coming. *(Eddy and Maggie exit)*

(As soon as they leave the toys open and then exit the toy box to center stage. They have been hiding behind the front of the box for the Eddie and Maggie lines.)

Sarge: *(out first)* Come on, soldiers, the coast is clear. You can disembark now. Hup, two, three, four.

Teddy: *(pokes head up)* Who made you the boss of us? What if I don't want to come out? What if I just want to sleep?

Astronaut: *(pushes past Teddy on to the stage)* Get out of the way, fuzzy. I want my last night as a toy to last.

Ninja: *(leaps from the box to land in a martial arts pose)* Last night as a toy? Why is this our last night as toys? I am a toy through and through and if I have to fight all the new toys, then so be it.

Astronaut: Fat chance of that. Tomorrow all the new toys will have taken our places and we will get bagged up in an old, stinky, garbage bag and dropped off at some collection box in a church parking lot. Enjoy it now, toys, for tomorrow we go back to the world of unloved, useless, and broken items.

Barbie: *(exits box)* No, no, no. Maggie loves me.

Astronaut: Love is fleeting in the world of toys, Babs.

Raggedy Ann: *(pops up and exits box)* Maggie loves me too.

Cowgirl: *(pops up and exits box)* Me too.

Astronaut: Love has nothing to do with Christmas.

Sarge: Be quiet, space cadet, you're scaring the girls.

Barbie: I would be the first to go. I have no arm. I will be stuffed in a bag and thrown away. *(begins to cry loudly)*

Teddy: Yeah, in a cold steel box in a lonely, isolated, church parking lot, left for mice to nibble at your toes. *(girls cry in unison)*

Sarge: Okay, okay, cut it out. That isn't the way it is. That isn't what Christmas is about. This is my fourth one. I have experience in these things. As you know, being Eddie's favorite, I got to go to the Christmas Eve service tonight. I learned a thing or two about Christmas.

(three girl toys run up to him)

Cowgirl: Like what?

Sarge: They sang songs about a baby being born in a place called Bethlehem. Let me start it and you can all join in.

SONG 1 *(any appropriate carol here)*

Raggedy Ann: Where's Bethlehem?

Teddy: I think it is in the living room right under the tree with all the lights on it. I saw this little set of people and one of them was a baby.

Ninja: Yes, one of the camels attempted to spit on me but I karate chopped him.

Barbie: Yuck! Sarge, what happened to the baby?

Sarge: Here is the story as I heard it. Remember that I am a simple soldier, so I have to tell a simple story. First of all, the baby's parents had to travel a long way to Bethlehem. Mary, the baby's mother, was almost ready to have the baby that they would name Jesus. Once they got into town there was no place for them to sleep.

Cowgirl: No toy box to sleep in?

Raggedy Ann: Not even room in Maggie's bed?

Sarge: They had to sleep in the barn along with donkeys, cows, and other things.

Cowgirl: Were there horses? Did they ride horses?

Sarge: I know there were donkeys and cows. The sheep were up on the hillside. Shepherds were keeping watch over the flocks that night.

SONG 2: "While Shepherds Watch Their Flocks" *(or something similar)*

Ninja: What happened next, Sarge? Did the sneaky ninja creep up on the shepherds?

Sarge: No, actually the shepherds weren't crept up on at all. In fact a bunch of angels appeared in the sky when Jesus was born and sang to them.

Astronaut: They flew up in the sky? It must be some of my relatives. Were they astronauts like me?

Raggedy Ann: What song did they sing?

Sarge: They sang "Joy To The World."

SONG 3: "Joy To The World"

Ninja: Remember that camel that spit at me under the tree with the lights? There were three of them and on the camels were three guys dressed like kings. Who were they?

Sarge: That is the best part of the story, at least for us toys, because it talks about us.

Barbie: Did it say Barbie?

Teddy: I am sure my name is mentioned because I am so cute and cuddly.

Astronaut: Pipe down everybody. Maybe there is hope for us yet. Maybe these three kings will save us from being shoved in an old bag and thrown away.

Sarge: The three kings came from far away carrying something.

SONG 4: "We Three Kings"

Sarge: They were carrying the first Christmas gifts and they gave them to the baby Jesus. That means that each one of us has a wonderful place in this story. We are gifts given at Christmas time. We're not just toys. This isn't a toy story. We are an important part of a *joy* story. We represent gifts that are given to boys and girls because Jesus was born on that first Christmas. You are special in this world today. My experience over the last three Christmases has taught me that the new toys don't replace us. They just join us to create more fun, more happiness, and more joy!

Astronaut: All because Jesus was born on that first Christmas morning.

SONG 5: "The First Noel"

Mom: *(voice from offstage)* John, I hear music coming from the playroom and I see a light under the door. The kids must have forgotten to shut everything off and put their toys away. I'll get it. *(enters the stage and all the toys freeze in place like statues)* I must have been hearing things. Oh my, they left their toys all over the floor. Christmas Eve will do that to kids. *(exits and turns off the lights)*

Toys: *(singing Song 5 as they go back into their box)*

Almost, Just Like Dickens' Christmas Carol

Approximate length: 20-25 minutes

Cast:

Abby Neezer — older girl from 14 to 17 (could be Andy Neezer)

Abby's cousin — girl or boy of any age but must be able to recite a few lines

Director — Sunday school teacher or older student

Marylee — same age (roughly) as Abby

Ghost of Christmas Past — boy or girl with ability to memorize and speak lines

Ghost of Christmas Present — Sunday school teacher or older boy dressed as Santa Claus

Ghost of Christmas Future — small child with no lines wearing an all black hooded robe or XXL black hoodie sweatshirt

Abby as a small child — youngest girl of small stature

Little girl or boy — able to recite lines

TV set cast:

    Director

    Camera Operator (no lines)

    Make-up (no lines)

    Guitar player

    Drummer (also plays Ghost of Christmas Present)

    Sound effects from backstage

Props:

2 Guitars

Drum set

Chains (plastic chain like for hanging lamps)
Small nativity set
Director's chair with a star on it
Large cardboard box with a TV painted on two opposite
    sides. One side has the words "It's Abby's World" writ-
    ten on it. The other side has the same but with the word
    Canceled written across "It's Abby's World."
Small Christmas tree
Foil icicles

Costumes:
Santa Claus suit
Winter scarves, hats, gloves for choir
Old dirty, torn shirts for choir
XXL black hooded sweatshirt or black hooded robe

Set:
The TV studio set for a children's TV show. A director's chair
sits to stage right (right side as you look at the platform).

Director: Everybody on the set. We are taping the scene where Abby sings "Joy To The World." Places everyone.

(Abby is center stage. Guitar player to her right and drums to her left. Kids do not play them but only act as if they are.)

Okay, Abby. Sing away.

Abby: *(sings very flat and totally without feeling)* Joy to the world, the Lord has come...

Director: Cut, cut, cut! Abby what was that? This is one of the most joyful songs of the Christmas season. You make it sound like you just lost your boyfriend. What's wrong?

Abby: Christmas? Bah, humbug!

Director: What do mean, Bah humbug? This is Christmas and everyone loves Christmas. My cat loves Christmas. My dog loves Christmas. Everyone, and I mean *everyone*, loves Christmas.

Abby: I don't. I don't like buying people gifts. I don't like buying gifts for people I don't really know, like Aunt Gertrude. She smells like mothballs and why should I buy her a gift? If the truth be known, I don't even enjoy buying gifts for people I like. The blinking colored lights give me a headache, and the malls are so terribly crowded this time of the year. When people say, "Merry Christmas," I say "Bah, humbug!"

Cousin: But Abby, our whole family loves Christmas. Don't you remember when we were kids, and how gifts were stacked from the floor to the ceiling at Gramma's?

Abby: Humbug, I say, bah, humbug!

Director: Maybe we should take a break. Everyone take five and then be back on the set in thirty minutes.

(all leave except Abby — she moves to the director's chair with a star on it; she sits and soon falls asleep, snoring loudly)

SFX: *pounding on a door and chains rattling*

Abby: Who's there? *(wakes and looks around the chair and under it, then sits down again)*

SFX: *rattling chains start again; heavy stomping footsteps*

Abby: Cut it out! Whoever is trying to scare me, just cut it out. I don't scare easily and remember, it is Christmas and not Halloween.

SFX: *rattling chains and heavy footsteps*

(Marylee enters stomping her feet and shaking her chains)

Marylee: *(character uses a very fake, spooky voice)* Do you remember me, Abby Neezer? I once walked on this earth next to you. We were known as the A and M Band, but today, you are a big TV star. Abby Neezer, do you remember me?

Abby: Yeah, you're my best friend. You live next door to me.

Marylee: I have come to warn you from my grave.

Abby: Warn me? The grave? What grave? Marylee, you're not dead. We just had lunch together.

Marylee: Wooooooh! *(starts in spooky voice but coughs and goes back to her normal voice)* I know, I know, but this gig pays better than babysitting. Just let me finish up so I can go home for dinner. All right?

Abby: Is this a dream?

Marylee: *(moans and rattles chains)* Today you will be visited by three ghosts.

Abby: I am way too busy today. It's Christmas Eve, you know. Can we move this to later in the week?

Marylee: *(rattles chains louder)* Sorry, gotta be tonight. Get ready for the ghosts. *(exits while still rattling chains)*

Abby: This has to be a dream. I need to rest. It is just the stress of the holidays getting to me. *(Ghost of Christmas Past enters and clears throat)*

Ghost of Christmas Past: It is I, the Ghost of Christmas Past!

Abby: *(startled awake)* You're the Ghost of Christmas Past? *(laughing)* You look a lot like my Sunday school teacher in a Santa suit.

Ghost of Christmas Past: I know, but this gig pays better and the suit was all there was left in wardrobe. Tonight we will look at your past Christmases.

(takes Abby's hand)

(three kids enter carrying gifts, wrapping paper, scissors, and tape)

Ghost of Christmas Past: Do you remember this day?

Abby: Yeah, that's me and my little sister and brother. We were wrapping our gifts for Mom and Dad. They were terrible wrappers but Mom and Dad loved the gifts even more.

Ghost of Christmas Past: Sometimes the Christmas spirit returns when you give to others.

(three kids exit)

(kids choir enters dressed in winter hats, scarves, and gloves)

Ghost of Christmas Past: Do you remember this day?

Abby: Wow, I sure do. All the kids in our Sunday school got together and we went to the nursing home where my grandmother is and we sang. That is one of my best memories of Christmas.

(kids choir softly sings a Christmas carol)

Abby: I sure miss those days.

Ghost of Christmas Past: Sometimes the Christmas spirit comes when you give of yourself to others. *(takes Abby back to her chair and Abby sits — the Ghost exits)*

(Ghost of Christmas Present enters carrying a small Christmas tree and some foil icicles)

Ghost of Christmas Present: Wake up, Abby. We have a lot to do and your dressing room isn't decorated yet. *(throws some foil icicles on Abby's head)*

Abby: What? I guess you must be the Ghost of Christmas Present.

Ghost of Christmas Present: Yes-sirree!

Abby: You look just like the drummer in my band on my TV show.

Ghost of Christmas Present: I know, but this gig pays better.

Abby: I better talk to my producer and see if I can't get a few raises for people around this place.

Ghost of Christmas Present: Let's decorate. *(throws icicles in the air)*

Abby: You're getting my dressing room all messy.

Ghost of Christmas Present: I guess we can decorate later but first I have some people I want you to meet.

(kids choir enters dressed in hole-ridden, dirty shirts and pants)

Ghost of Christmas Present: You were supposed to sing at their Orphanage Christmas party tonight but you broke that promise, so you could get your nails done. Just to show you how nice and sweet they are, the orphans decided to sing to you.

(kids choir sings a brief Christmas carol)

Ghost of Christmas Present: They were so good but most of them shivered through that song because they had no coats to wear.

Abby: I guess I could go through my closet and see what's out of style and give it to them.

Ghost of Christmas Present: Jesus said, "For as much as you do for the least of these then you do it to me."

Abby: I'll give them some old tennis shoes too.

Ghost of Christmas Present: We must leave you now.

(Ghost of Christmas Present and choir sings a carol quietly as they leave. Abby returns to her chair)

Abby: I guess I've become a bit selfish lately. I may have lost my heart but look at this TV set. I'm a big star. I still have that. Kids still love me when I'm on TV.

(Ghost of Christmas Future enters and Abby does a double-take when she sees him)

Abby: You must be the Ghost of Christmas Future. I kinda thought you would be taller than that.

(Ghost of Christmas Future points. As he points three kids enter and sit on the floor. A fourth child enters with a cardboard box painted like a TV set. Inside the screen it says, "It's Abby's World.")

Kid 1: I don't like this show anymore.

Kid 2: Me either.

Kid 3: Let's just go outside and play.

Abby: My ratings have been dropping. *(with her forefinger to her chin she says)* Look at the bright side, I am at least getting them outside to play. That's got to count for something.

(Child in TV Box turns around. On the back is the same TV with "It's Abby's World" on it but now there is a canceled sticker across it)

Abby: Ghost of Christmas Future, is that what will happen or is this just what could happen if I don't turn my heart back and find the meaning of Christmas again?

(Ghost of Christmas Future exits)

Abby: Wow! I guess I don't even know what Christmas is all about anymore. *(goes back to her chair and sits)*

(little girl or little boy enters)

Little Girl or Boy: Aren't you Abby from that TV show?

Abby: Yeah. Are you another ghost?

Little Girl or Boy: Nope. I'm a real person and I need some help.

Abby: Sure, what is it? Now, that I'm canceled I guess I have a lot of time.

Little Girl or Boy: I have to set up these pieces for the manger scene, but I don't know what goes where or who is who. Can you help me make the Christmas story?

Abby: Well, yeah. I sure can. Let me see what you have there. *(holds up the three wise men)* These are the wise men and they brought gifts. *(holds up a shepherd)* This guy is a shepherd. The angels appeared to him and sang to him. *(holds up Joseph)* This is Joseph. He is Mary's husband and he was very kind to Mary on their trip to Bethlehem. *(holds up Mary)* This is Mary. She gave birth to... I can't find Jesus. Where's Jesus?

Little Girl or Boy: I know where he is. You are just kidding me because you know where he is too.

Abby: Where is he? *(frantically looks around)*

Little Girl or Boy: In our hearts. He lives in our hearts because of Christmas day.

(director and other cast members enter)

Director: Everyone, back on the set. *(to Abby)* I've written out the "Joy To The World" song so you won't have to sing it, Abby.

Abby: Are you kidding me? I have to sing it. My little friend just reminded me of the real meaning of Christmas. Now I can sing "Joy To The World" with the joy of Christmas in my heart.

(all the cast sings "Joy To The World")

Older Child 2: Christmas isn't about big houses with lights all over them. In fact, Jesus was born in a barn.

Older Child 1: *(sarcastically)* Yeah, right. Jesus was born in a barn. I don't believe that one.

Child 1: I'm joining your club too. I may live in a big house but I feel like my parents have forgotten what Christmas is really about, and to be honest, I don't think I ever knew what it was about.

Older Child 2: But it isn't about big houses. Don't you remember the song "Away In The Manger"? It tells us that Jesus was born in a barn. Sing it and you'll remember.

Children: *(sing together)*

Song 1: "Away In The Manger"

Child 3: The song is right. Christmas isn't about big houses. I'm quitting the "I Hate Christmas" Club.

Child 4: Me too.

Child 5: Me, three.

Older Child 1: *(throws his arms in the air to show surrender)* So Jesus was born in a manger and in a barn but I still hate Christmas. I am still the president of the "I Hate Christmas" Club. Every year at Christmastime, all I see are a bunch of stressed out and angry adults. They get mad when they wait in lines at stores. They get mad when they can't find a parking spot. They are grouchy all the time. None of them are happy. Christmas doesn't make people happy. Who wants to join my "I Hate Christmas" Club?

Child 3: I want to rejoin.

Child 4: Me too.

Child 5: Me, three.

(Children 3, 4, and 5 stand up again and move close to Older Child 1)

Child 9: I am still a solid and convinced member of the club. Lead on Mr. President. When do I get my T-shirt?

Older Child 1: *(frustrated)* There are no T-shirts!

Older Child 2: I guess you missed one of the central messages of Christmas. Even the angels sang about it when Jesus was born. Jesus wasn't born so we could all be angry and grouchy. He was born so we could be happy.

Child 2: How do you know that?

Older Child 2: We sing about in church. Remember the song "Joy To The World"? That is what the angels sang when Jesus was born. Sing it and you will remember.

Children: *(sing together)*

Song 2: "Joy To The World"

Older Child 1: All right, all right, I will give you that one too. Big deal, so Christmas is supposed to be about joy. No

Elf Elementary

Approximate length: 20-25 minutes

Characters:
Teacher Miss Snow
Mrs. Claus
Elf Students, however many you need

Props:
Each elf should have a similar costume. These can be as simple as an elf hat, Santa hat, or each of them simply dressed in green. The pointed ears are nice but might get too difficult with younger children and with budgets.

Sunday school chairs or desks set up in rows that stagger so each child can be seen by the congregation.

A small podium for the teacher

Teacher should have on a green dress or green outfit. This can be played by an older child or by a Sunday school teacher.

Mrs. Claus should be in a red outfit trimmed in white fur.

Make sure there are microphones placed conveniently between the students to pick up their voices. Kids are notoriously quiet when you want them to be loud.

(The kids are horsing around in class. No one is in their seat. At Miss Snow's first word, each child quickly jumps in their seat and folds their hands across their laps.)

Miss Snow: Sorry I am late, children. *(looks at her class notes and doesn't notice the mayhem until all the children are in their seats; allow your best class clown to be the last in his or her seat; once all of them plop down the children should give the most angelic of looks)* My goodness, you are such a well-behaved class today. Is it because today is the *big* day?

All Elf Children: *(in unison)* Good morning, Miss Snow! How are you today?

Miss Snow: Did I walk into the wrong classroom? What did you do to all of my students? *(looks around and then gestures with her finger)* Oh, I get it. You all remembered that Mrs. Santa Claus is coming today to speak to the class.

Elf 1: *(Elf 1 raises hand and Miss Snow points to recognize that he/she is allowed to speak)* Is she bringing candy canes? Do we get to taste all the Christmas cookies that Santa didn't eat?

Miss Snow: I really don't know what Mrs. Claus has in mind for her talk today. We will see what she brings or has to say in a few minutes but first let's practice our song. A special thanks to Emily Elf for her rewriting of the lyrics. Let's try it now.

Elves and Miss Snow: *(sing together)*

SONG 1: "Mrs. Claus Is Comin' To Class"
You better watch out
You better not cry
You better not pout
I'm telling you why
Mrs. Claus is coming to class

She'll be looking at our heads
Checking us for lice;
Gonna find out who's teasing the mice
Mrs. Claus is coming to class

She sees you when you're talking
She pinches to keep you awake
She knows if you've been bad or good
So be good for goodness sake

You better watch out
You better not cry
You better not pout
I'm telling you why
Mrs. Claus is coming to class

Emily Elf: *(jumps up)* Hey, those aren't the words I wrote.

Eddie Elf: I know, I thought your lyrics were lame so I re-wrote them. Pretty good, if I do say so myself.

Emily Elf: My lyrics were not lame. They were not naughty like yours but nice. Mrs. Claus will like mine better.

Miss Snow: We won't have time to find out. Mrs. Claus is at the door now so let's just skip the song and hope she didn't hear that last version.

Mrs. Claus: Good morning, elves.

Elves: *(in unison)* Good morning, Mrs. Claus.

Mrs. Claus: Do any of you know why I am here this morning?

Emily Elf: *(raises her hand then Miss Snow points to her)* To hear the great lyrics to the song I wrote before Eddie Elf destroyed it with his dumb words.

Eddie Elf: I think the other elves liked my version better. Didn't you, fellow elves?

Elves: *(in unison except Emily)* Yep, we sure did.

Miss Snow: That's enough. I am so sorry, Mrs. Claus. They were absolutely perfect until just a moment ago.

Mrs. Claus: Elves will be elves, Miss Snow. Mr. Claus and I have seen enough of them over the years to know that they can be fun and funny. So, can someone tell me why I am here?

Elf 2: *(to the neighboring Elf 3)* If she doesn't know then how are we supposed to know?

Elf 3: *(shrugs)* I don't know.

Elf 4: *(waves hand furiously in the air)* I know, I know, I know, I know.

Miss Snow: Go ahead, tell Mrs. Claus.

Elf 4: Uh, uh, uh, uh.

Miss Snow: Did you forget what you wanted to say?

Elf 4: Uh-huh. *(nods head "yes")*

Mrs. Claus: That's all right because today I want to tell you the truth about Christmas.

Elf 5: *(to neighboring elf)* Oh, no. She's going to tell us that we are imaginary.

Elf 6: I wish you were imaginary.

Elf 7: I used to have an imaginary friend.

Elf 8: What happened to him?

Elf 7: He quit believing in me.

Elf 1: Does the story involve candy canes or Christmas cookies?

Mrs. Claus: No, but it does have animals, a baby, and a golden gift. It is a wonderful story and now that you are all old enough, it is time to tell you the truth. It is time for you to know why Mr. Claus and I do what we do every year and why we try to bring joy to every girl and boy in the world.

Elf 9: Why haven't we ever heard the story before?

Mrs. Claus: Oh, you have. You just didn't recognize it. Sometimes the truth is right in front of us but we just can't see it.

Elf 10: Like a ghost?

Emily Elf: There are no ghosts. That is not a nice thing to say in front of Mrs. Claus.

Mrs. Claus: That is okay, Emily Elf. That is why I am here. I want to explain things to all of you. As I was saying, the truth has been right there in front of you. In fact, you've been singing about it for most of your young lives. Let me show you. Does anyone know the Christmas carol "Away In A Manger"?

Elf 4: *(waves hand furiously in the air)* I know, I know, I know, I know!

Miss Snow: Go ahead and lead us in the song.

Elf 4: Uh, uh, uh, uh.

Emily Elf: You don't know it, do you?

Elf 4: I don't know it but if you help me then I can learn it.

Mrs. Claus: I know what we will do. Let us all sing it together so we can learn the song.

Elves: *(sing together)*

SONG 2: "Away In The Manger"

Mrs. Claus: That was beautiful, elves. As you can see, the truth about Christmas is right there in front of us. Christmas is all about a baby born in a manger. Joseph and Mary were traveling to Joseph's hometown when Mary's child decided

60

it was time to greet the world. Unfortunately, there was no hotel or motel rooms or hospitals so her baby was born in a barn.

Eddie Elf: I guess the baby's mother never asked him if he was born in a barn like my mother asks me when I leave the door open.

Mrs. Claus: No, she probably never did ask him that. Can someone tell me who that baby is?

Elf 4: *(waves arm in air wildly)* I know, I know, I know, I know.

Elf 5: No, you don't.

Elf 4: I do, I do, I do, I do.

Miss Snow: Go ahead and answer then.

Elf 4: Uh, uh, uh, uh…

Elf 6: Not again.

Elf 4: It was Jesus! Jesus was born in a manger.

Elf 7: *(with an English accent)* By Jove, I think she's (he's) got it.

Mrs. Claus: Yes s/he does. But that isn't all of the story. There was a great choir that sang. Do you know who was in the choir?

Elf 8: I just hope it wasn't Mrs. Elfina, she has a terrible voice. I have to cover my ears where she sings. It reminds me of the time I stepped on my cat's tail. It hurts my ears just to remember.

Elf 9: Or Mr. Pointyears. He sounds like one of those frog toys my dad makes.

Mrs. Claus: You know who was in the choir. Remember the truth is right in front of you. All of you have sung the song, "Angels We Have Heard On High." Let's sing that one together.

Elves: *(sing together)*

SONG 3: "Angels We Have Heard On High"

Emily Elf: That song says the choir was made up of angels. Wow, Mrs. Claus, this is some great story but why do we give gifts to one another at Christmas time? Why do all the elves make toys for good little girls and boys?

Mrs. Claus: It was because of three very important men.

Elf 9: I know who that was. It was the three wise men. They were kings and it took them two years to find Jesus by following a star.

Elf 10: How did you know that?

Elf 9: The truth was right there in front of me. My dad and his two brothers always sing the song "We Three Kings" on Christmas morning. Now, I know what it means.

Mrs. Claus: That is correct. I am so proud of how all of you are beginning to see the story unfold. The three kings brought him gifts of gold, frankincense, and myrrh. Can we sing that song together?

Elves: *(sing together)*

SONG 4: "We Three Kings"

Eddie Elf: I know why they would bring gold and incense, but why bring a hot dog?

Mrs. Claus: A hotdog? What do you mean, Eddie?

Eddie Elf: You said they brought him a frank. That's a hot-dog at my dinner table. Why did they bring him a hotdog?

Elf 10: They didn't bring a frank or a hotdog. They brought frankincense. People made incense out of frankincense.

Eddie Elf: I think I understand now but what is myrrh?

Mrs. Claus: It is a perfume used to anoint kings. In fact all these gifts were traditionally given to newborn kings. It was a sign that these three wise men, or three kings, recognized Jesus as the king of heaven. They brought gifts and that is why Mr. Claus and I have been bringing gifts to children for all these years. On Jesus' birthday we bring gifts so everyone can remember that Jesus was born and he brought joy to the world. In fact, can you sing that song for me?

Elves: *(sing together)*

SONG 5: "Joy To The World"

Elf 1: What happened to Jesus after the Christmas story?

Elf 5: Did he go on and sit on a big throne?

Mrs. Claus: Yes, he is still on a big throne and rules in heaven. Before that though, Jesus grew up and became a man. Many people followed him and believed that he was the Son of God. Others, though, did not believe he was our Savior. Instead, they plotted to have him killed. Jesus was crucified on a cross and then he died and was buried.

Elf 8: That's a sad ending to the story.

Mrs. Claus: That wasn't the end. The end is so exciting and filled with so much joy, happiness, and hope that I wish I could tell it to you today but I believe you have recess now. Instead, I will plan to come back and tell you the rest of the story on Easter Sunday. How does that sound?

Elf 6: Great!

Miss Snow: Gather your coats and boots for recess but make sure you are back for the bell because we have another guest after recess.

Mrs. Claus: You will like this next guest.

(the sound of a Santa "Ho, Ho, Ho" is heard offstage)

Elf 1: Are there any candy canes or Christmas cookies involved with the next guest?

Mrs. Claus: There are always candy canes and Christmas cookies wherever this guest goes.